BRITAIN: THE FACTS

Government

Christopher Riches

FRANKLIN WATTS
LONDON·SYDNEY

First published in 2008
by Franklin Watts

Copyright © 2008 Christopher Riches and Trevor Bounford

Design by bounford.com

Franklin Watts
338 Euston Road
London NW1 3BH

Franklin Watts Australia
Level 17/207 Kent Street
Sydney, NSW 2000

All words in **bold** can be found in Glossary on pages 30–31. Website information is correct at time of going to press. However, the publishers cannot accept liability for any information or links found on third-party websites.

ISBN 978 0 7496 8382 5

Dewey classification: 320.941

Printed in China

Franklin Watts is a division of Hachette Children's Books, an Hachette Livre UK company.
www.hachettelivre.co.uk

Picture credits

The publishers would like to thank the following organisations for their kind permission to reproduce illustrations in this book:

Cover image © 2008 Paul Hughes/fotoLibra. p.5 Deryc Sands (photographer), Parliamentary copyright, reproduced with permission of Parliament; p.6 Reuters/Stephen Hird; p.9 (middle) Deryc Sands (photographer), Parliamentary copyright, reproduced with permission of Parliament; p.10 Deryc Sands (photographer), Parliamentary copyright, reproduced with permission of Parliament; p.12 Museum of London; p.13 Ackermann and Johnson; p.15 Leon Neal/AFP; p.16 (top) bounford.com; (middle) © Econ Engineering Ltd.; (bottom) © Westminster City Council; p.18 © Belfast City Council; p.19 (top) © Hartlepool Football Club; (middle) © Hartlepool Council; p.20 (centre) © National Museums Scotland. Licensor www.scran.ac.uk; (left) Scottish Parliamentary copyright material is reproduced with the permission of the Queen's Printer for Scotland on behalf of the Scottish Parliamentary Corporate Body; p.22 (top) © Welsh Assembly Government; (middle) © National Assembly for Wales Commission; p.23 © National Assembly for Wales Commission; p.24 (top) © Northern Ireland Assembly Commission; (bottom) © 2008 Brendan Montgomery/ fotoLibra; p.27 (top) Photo Service, European Parliament.

Maps and diagrams on pages 7, 9, 12, 13, 17, 19, 21, 23, 25 and 26, © bounford.com.

Contents

The British Constitution

A **constitution** defines how an organisation works. Most countries have a written constitution, but Britain does not. Our system of government has developed over hundreds of years and is based on many **Acts of Parliament** and legal decisions. There is no one single document that defines how Britain is governed.

The name of the country

The official title is the United Kingdom of Great Britain and Northern Ireland. This is shortened to the United Kingdom. Britain or Great Britain describes the island that contains England, Wales and Scotland but not Northern Ireland.

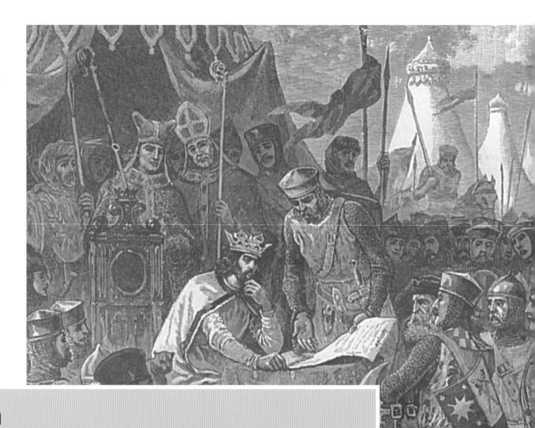

The Magna Carta

The King used to be all powerful. In 1215 King John, who was unpopular with his nobles, was forced to sign the Magna Carta (Latin for the Great Charter), which guaranteed certain rights to the people of England. One clause reads:

'We will appoint as justices, constables, sheriffs, or other officials, only men that know the law of the realm and are minded to keep it well.'

Another reads:
'There shall be standard measures of wine, ale, and corn (the London quarter), throughout the kingdom.'

The three elements of the constitution

The monarchy

- ▦ Head of State.
- ▦ Gives Royal **assent** to Acts of Parliament.
- ▦ A ceremonial role without political power.

Parliament

- ▦ Contains the **House of Commons** and the **House of Lords**.
- ▦ Supremacy over making, changing and abolishing laws.
- ▦ Government formed by **Members of Parliament**.
- ▦ House of Commons dominant.
- ▦ Members of House of Commons elected by the people.
- ▦ House of Lords mainly appointed.

The judiciary

- ▦ Administers justice in criminal and civil **courts**.
- ▦ Implements and interprets laws passed by Parliament.
- ▦ Independent of the government.

The State Opening of Parliament

At the start of each Parliamentary sitting (usually about once a year), the Monarch comes to Parliament. Members of both Houses of Parliament go to the House of Lords to hear the Monarch's speech. Written by the **Prime Minister**, it outlines what the government wishes to do in the following session of Parliament. The Monarch speaks from the throne in the House of Lords.

'Black Rod' (below) is an official of the House of Lords. He goes to the House of Commons to bring members to the House of Lords to hear the Monarch's speech. The Monarch cannot enter the House of Commons.

The Government

The government is formed by the political party that has the largest number of members of the House of Commons. The government is led by the Prime Minister, who heads that political party.

The Cabinet

The **Cabinet** is the group of senior **ministers** in the government. It decides on the policy of the government. Each minister is responsible for a particular part of the government. Three hundred years ago, the king's advisers would meet to consider the matters of the day. They met in a small, private room, which, at that time, was called a 'cabinet'. Today there are 22 Cabinet ministers and the Cabinet meets every Thursday morning at 10 Downing Street, the home of the Prime Minister.

Each member of the Cabinet has particular responsibilities. Some Cabinet titles have a long history:

The Chancellor of the Exchequer looks after the country's finances. The Exchequer was first described around 1180 and its name comes from the chequered tablecloth that, with counters, was used to keep a record of state accounts.

The Lord Privy Seal was originally the person responsible for keeping the king's private seal (a wax image of the seal was attached to documents to make them official). This is now combined with the position of Leader of the House of Commons. It was once said that the holder of the office was 'neither a Lord, nor a privy, nor a seal'.

The Prime Minister, Gordon Brown, chairing a Cabinet meeting.

Government departments

Government departments carry out the policies of the government. The staff in the departments are called **civil servants**. They are politically neutral. As well as the main departments listed below, there are many other organisations funded by the government that help administer the country. Some are called Non-Departmental Public Bodies, better known as 'Quangos'.

The main government departments are:

- Business, Enterprise and Regulatory Reform
- Children, Schools and Families
- Communities and Local Government
- Culture, Media and Sport
- Defence
- Environment, Food and Rural Affairs
- Foreign and Commonwealth Office
- Health
- Her Majesty's Treasury
- Home Office
- Innovations, Universities and Skills
- International Development
- Justice
- Northern Ireland Office
- Scotland Office
- Transport
- Wales Office
- Work and Pensions

Sometimes government and government departments are referred to as '**Whitehall**'. Originally White Hall was a Royal palace. All that remains of the palace is the Banqueting House, built in 1619. Charles I was executed in 1649 outside this building. Whitehall is now the name of the road close to the Houses of Parliament where the main government departments are. The Houses of Parliament are often referred to as '**Westminster**'. They are on the site of the Palace of Westminster, another Royal palace.

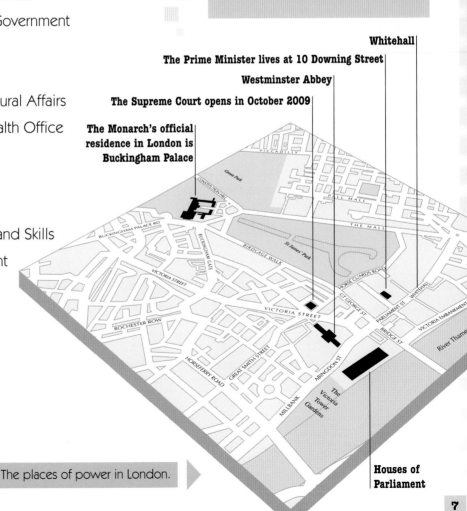

Whitehall

The Prime Minister lives at 10 Downing Street

Westminster Abbey

The Supreme Court opens in October 2009

The Monarch's official residence in London is Buckingham Palace

The places of power in London.

Houses of Parliament

The House of Commons

The House of Commons is the more important of the two Houses of Parliament. It is responsible for approving government expenditure and taxation and for all new laws. It is made up of 646 Members of Parliament (MPs). Each member is elected by the people who live in a particular area, called a **constituency**. There are 646 constituencies in Britain. This number can change with population changes. The political party with most members forms the government.

What happens in the Commons

Making laws

🏛 The government puts forward new laws in Parliamentary **Bills**. These are discussed and voted upon.

Asking questions

🏛 Each week the Prime Minister spends 30 minutes answering questions from Members of Parliament. This is called Prime Minister's Question Time.

🏛 On a regular basis other Ministers answer questions relating to their department.

Detailed investigation

🏛 The House of Commons Select Committees investigate government policy and matters of public concern. They can call experts to give evidence.

> The **Speaker** ensures that Members speak politely. Recent words used by MPs to describe one another that the Speaker has objected to include: coward, guttersnipe, hooligan, rat, swine, stoolpigeon and traitor.

The House of Commons time line

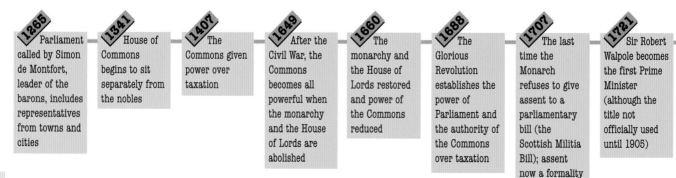

1265 Parliament called by Simon de Montfort, leader of the barons, includes representatives from towns and cities

1341 House of Commons begins to sit separately from the nobles

1407 The Commons given power over taxation

1649 After the Civil War, the Commons becomes all powerful when the monarchy and the House of Lords are abolished

1660 The monarchy and the House of Lords restored and power of the Commons reduced

1688 The Glorious Revolution establishes the power of Parliament and the authority of the Commons over taxation

1707 The last time the Monarch refuses to give assent to a parliamentary bill (the Scottish Militia Bill); assent now a formality

1721 Sir Robert Walpole becomes the first Prime Minister (although the title not officially used until 1905)

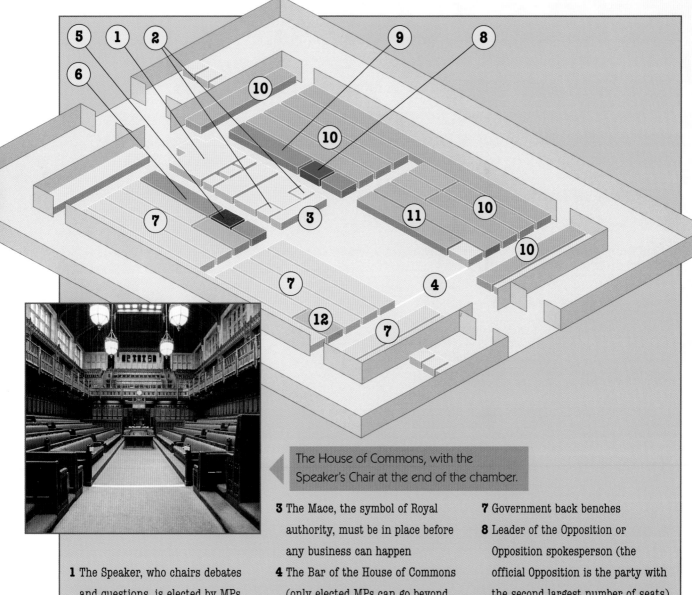

The House of Commons, with the Speaker's Chair at the end of the chamber.

1 The Speaker, who chairs debates and questions, is elected by MPs from amongst themselves and is impartial

2 Dispatch Boxes (originally boxes for holding official papers), used as paper rests by official speakers

3 The Mace, the symbol of Royal authority, must be in place before any business can happen

4 The Bar of the House of Commons (only elected MPs can go beyond this point)

5 Prime Minister or Government spokesperson

6 The Government front **bench** (for ministers)

7 Government back benches

8 Leader of the Opposition or Opposition spokesperson (the official Opposition is the party with the second largest number of seats)

9 The Opposition front bench (for 'Shadow' ministers)

10 Opposition back benches

11 Liberal Democrats

12 Other smaller Parties

1832 The first Reform Act increases the number of men who can vote in elections

1902 Lord Salisbury, the last Prime Minister to sit in the House of Lords, resigns, strengthening the power of the Commons

1911 The Parliament Act stops the Lords rejecting a Bill passed in the Commons

1918 Votes first given to women over 30 and to all men over 21

1978 First radio broadcast from the Commons

1989 First television broadcast from the Commons

1997 The first Muslim MP, Mohammed Sarwar, elected by Glasgow Govan

1999 Devolution of certain powers to Scotland, Wales and Northern Ireland

The House of Lords

The second chamber of Parliament is called the House of Lords.
Its members are not elected. Reform of the House of Lords has started,
but no agreement can be reached on how to complete the reform.

The House of Lords:

- modifies laws proposed by the House of Commons.
  Any change it makes has to be approved by the House of Commons.
- proposes new laws for the House of Commons to consider.
- has no authority over financial matters.
- is also the highest Court in Britain. In 2009 this power transfers to a
  new Supreme Court, independent of the House of Lords.

Who sits in the House of Lords?

Hereditary peers. Originally nobles (Lords or peers) created by the Monarch. They were not elected. When a noble died, his eldest son **inherited** the right to sit in the House of Lords. Until 1958 all peers were hereditary. In recent reforms, their numbers have been reduced from over 700 to 92.

Archbishops and bishops. There are 2 archbishops and 24 bishops from the Church of England. The most senior is the Archbishop of Canterbury.

Life peers. Since 1958, individuals who have made notable contributions to society have been appointed Life peers. Their position in the House of Lords cannot

The House of Lords, with the Monarch's throne (top). Peers sit on three sides. The Speaker sits on the Woolsack in front of the throne. The day starts with questions to government ministers on policies and current issues.

be passed on to members of their families. There are now around 600 Life peers.

Law lords. The most senior judges. When the Supreme Court opens (from 2009), they will no longer have seats in the House of Lords.

The Woolsack

The Speaker of the House of Lords sits on the Woolsack. This is not a normal chair, but a large sack stuffed with wool. In the early days of Parliament, wool was Britain's most valuable item of trade and so it was a symbol of the wealth of the country. Today, the Woolsack is stuffed with wool from all over the **Commonwealth**.

The Gunpowder Plot

On 5 November 1605 King James I was going to the House of Lords for the State Opening of Parliament. A group opposed to the King's rule planned to blow up Parliament. They had rented a basement store below the House of Lords and had put 36 barrels of gunpowder there. One of the gang, Guy Fawkes, was with the gunpowder and would have set it off on the day. However, the authorities were tipped off and Guy Fawkes and his barrels were found on the night of 4 November. The plot failed and the conspirators were executed. We celebrate the defeat of the plot on 5 November every year with fireworks and bonfires – and on the bonfires we burn 'Guys', named after Guy Fawkes.

General Elections

A **General Election** is held at least every five years. Everyone over 18 has the opportunity to **vote** for a Member of Parliament to represent them in the House of Commons. It is the way we chose who should govern us and for the political parties to explain what their priorities are.

How does the system work?

In each constituency, individuals representing political parties **stand** for **election**. A voter places a **X** against the name of their chosen **candidate** on a **ballot paper**. The votes cast for each candidate are then added up. The candidate with the most votes wins. This is called the **first-past-the-post system**.

For the General Election in 2005, the UK was divided into 646 constituencies. A constituency has around 70,000 voters.

The political party that wins the largest number of seats is then asked by the Monarch to form a government. If an MP resigns or dies between elections, a **by-election** is held. This is an election that is held just in that constituency.

Constituencies	
● England	529
● Scotland	59
● Wales	40
● Northern Ireland	18
United Kingdom	**total 646**

The right to vote

Up to 1832 Only a limited number of men could vote, based on land ownership and some ancient rights

1832 Voting rights extended to include men who owned their houses. Abolition of rotten boroughs

1867 Voting rights extended to many working men

1918 Votes given to all men over 21 and women over 30. Number of voters increased from 8 million to 21 million.

Is the voting system fair?

In these charts the inner ring shows the share of the vote each party received in three General Elections. The outer ring shows the number of MPs. Look at the Liberal Democrats in 1983 and at the Labour and Conservative share and seats in 2005. Does the system seem fair?

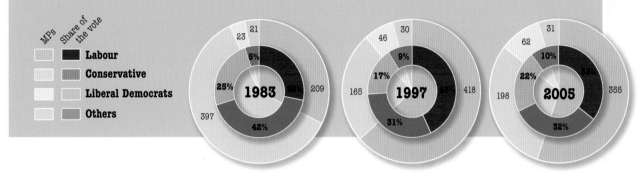

MPs

Share of the vote

- **Labour**
- **Conservative**
- **Liberal Democrats**
- **Others**

1983
21
23
5%
25%
23%
209
397
42%

1997
30
46
9%
17%
46%
165
418
31%

2005
31
62
10%
22%
35%
198
355
32%

A rotten borough

Now everyone who is aged 18 or over can vote for a Member of Parliament. Before 1832, some constituencies, called 'rotten boroughs', had so few voters that they could be **bribed**. Dunwich, in Suffolk, had two MPs but only 32 voters. Once it was the largest port in East Anglia but it had mostly fallen into the sea, and only a small village was left.

A suffragette being led away by the police. Suffragettes campaigned to get votes for women by holding demonstrations and taking direct action.

1926
Voting age for women reduced to 21

1969
Voting age reduced to 18 for everyone

FACTS

Largest majority: 62,253 for Sir Cooper Rawsom, Brighton, 1931

Smallest majority: 1 for Mark Oaten, Winchester, 1997, and for A. J. Flint, Derbyshire Ilkeston, 1931.

Fewest votes for a candidate: 1 for Catherine Taylor-Dawson, Vote for Yourself Rainbow Dream Ticket candidate, Cardiff North, 2005

Longest serving MP: Sir Winston Churchill (right), 61 years

Largest constituency: Ross, Skye and Lochaber in Scotland – 31,000 square kilometres

Smallest constituency: Islington North in London – 8 square kilometres

Political Parties

People who believe that the country should be governed in a particular way form political parties. The parties put forward candidates at local and national elections.

Political parties started in the eighteenth century. Two important groups were the Whigs and the Tories.

- The Whigs were named after a band of Scottish rebels who opposed Charles I in 1648 and were called whiggamores.
- The Tories were named after Irish peasants who had lost their land to English settlers and became robbers.

Over time the Whigs became the Liberal Party (and then the Liberal Democrats). The Tories became the Conservative Party.

All political parties use the internet to tell people about themselves and recruit members.

Not all political parties are the same. Have you heard of the Official Monster Raving Loony Party? It was founded by Screaming 'Lord' Sutch in 1983. He stood for election 42 times! Among current policies being considered are:

! all new homes should be built with a swimming pool and bouncy castle as standard

! it should be illegal to wake up before 9 a.m.

They have never won an election!

- The Labour Party was formed in 1906. It grew out of a wish to see **trade unionists** and working people elected as MPs. Keir Hardie, elected an MP in 1891, became the first leader of the Labour Party.

How is a party organised?

A political party is made up of people who support the policies of the party. Members join a local branch and can then take part in:

- selecting candidates for election at local and national level.

Political parties and recent General Elections

	2005	1997	1983
	MPs		
Labour Party	355	418	209
Conservative Party	198	165	397
Liberal Democrats	62	46	23
Democratic Unionist Party	9	2	3
Scottish National Party	6	6	2
Sinn Fein	5	2	1
Independents	4	3	2
Plaid Cymru (the Party of Wales)	3	4	2
Social Democratic and Labour Party	3	3	1
Ulster Unionist Party	1	10	11

None of the big parties stand for election in Northern Ireland. Instead the parties involved are the Democratic Unionist Party, Sinn Fein, Social Democratic and Labour Party and the Ulster Unionist Party.

Left Wing – Right Wing

These terms are used to describe political parties. In 1789, at the start of the French Revolution, those Assembly members who wanted equal rights for all sat on the left of the President of the Assembly, while those with traditional views sat on the right. In Britain Labour was seen as left wing, Conservatives right wing and the Liberal Democrats in the centre. Today many people argue that everyone is in the centre!

- electing the leader of the party.
- debating and forming party policies.
- campaigning for their candidates at elections.

Each party has an annual conference where policy is debated. Each member pays a **subscription**. Individuals, companies and trade unions also give money. Some suggest that these **donations** may buy political influence.

Gordon Brown addressing the Labour Party Conference. The conference is held every year in September. It helps to decide Labour Party policy on many issues.

Local Government

The government at Westminster decides on national issues. However, there are many things that need to be decided at a local level, from when the rubbish is collected to whether a new building should be allowed. These matters are all the responsibility of local government.

Key services that local government is responsible for include:

- Arts and culture
- Education: from nurseries to colleges of further education
- Environment
- Housing
- All roads, except motorways and some major roads
- Planning: deciding on what can be built and where
- Rubbish collection: when it should be collected and how much should be recycled
- Social welfare: helping families, the sick and the elderly
- Sports facilities

Local government receives most of its money from central government. It also raises taxes locally. This is done with the **Council Tax**, a tax based on the value of people's houses. Each **council** can charge a different amount. The average in England is £1,373 per house for one year.

Collecting the rubbish, keeping the roads safe and providing swimming pools are all examples of services a council provides.

How is local government organised?

The country is divided into many areas for local government. In Scotland, Wales and Northern Ireland, each area is covered by a single local government council (see pages 20–25). In England it is more complicated. In some places there are two levels of local government. A District looks after certain services, such as rubbish collection and planning, while the County looks after services such as education. In other areas, there is a single council. In big cities this is called a Metropolitan borough and in other areas it is called a Unitary council.

In England there are:

Counties	34
Districts	238
Metropolitan boroughs	36
London boroughs	33
Unitary councils	47

The counties of England are some of the oldest units of local government in the world – Hampshire was recorded in the year 757. Some county names continue to be used, even though they no longer have a government role. Middlesex and Westmorland are examples.

The smallest county is Rutland. It has a population of 38,000 people and contains no large towns. It was abolished as a county in 1974 but was reinstated as a Unitary council in 1997. Its motto is 'Much in little'.

This is the County of Lancashire. It has 12 Districts

This is the District of Ribble Valley

This is the Unitary Council of Warrington

This is the Metropolitan borough of Manchester. It is one of the 10 Metropolitan boroughs that make up Greater Manchester

Who Runs Local Government?

Councils are run by elected **councillors**. They meet regularly to decide what the council should do. They are advised by full-time council officials.

Who becomes a councillor?

There are over 21,000 elected councillors on 410 different local authorities in England. Each councillor represents a particular geographical area called a ward. Councillors are elected every four years by the people who live in the ward.

Mayors

The **mayor** of a town or city is a councillor selected to do many official duties for the council – opening buildings, visiting schools, entertaining important visitors. The mayor usually wears a chain of office.

In recent years, some cities have elected a mayor who is active in running the city. The Mayor of London is the most well-known.

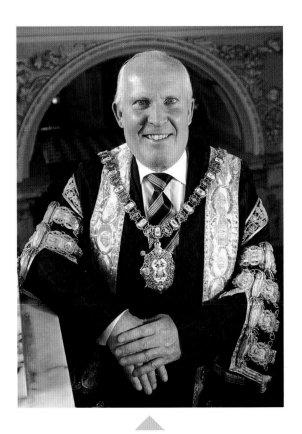

A mayor in his official robes. Note the chain of office that he wears around his neck.

Politics and local government

Political parties are very active in local government and control most councils. In addition there are **independent** councillors who think that party politics should not be part of local government. A few authorities are run by independent councillors.

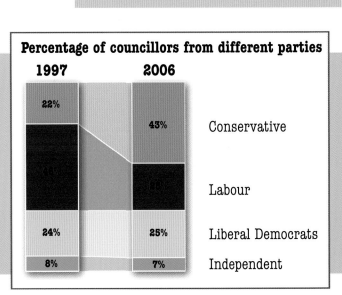

Percentage of councillors from different parties

1997	2006	
22%	43%	Conservative
		Labour
24%	25%	Liberal Democrats
8%	7%	Independent

FACTS

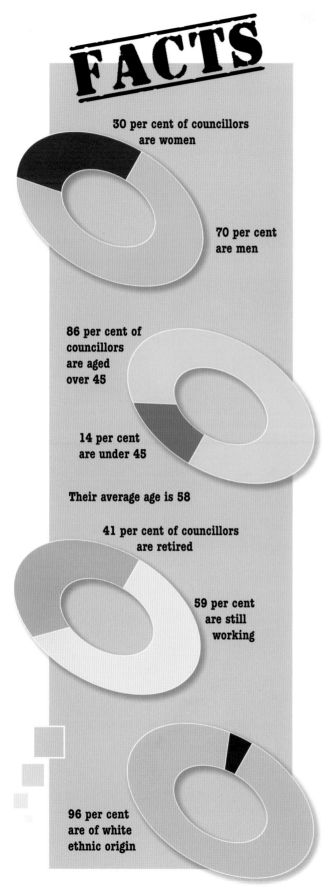

30 per cent of councillors are women

70 per cent are men

86 per cent of councillors are aged over 45

14 per cent are under 45

Their average age is 58

41 per cent of councillors are retired

59 per cent are still working

96 per cent are of white ethnic origin

H'Angus the Monkey

In 2002 there was an election for the Mayor of Hartlepool. One of the candidates was Stuart Drummond, better known locally as the mascot of Hartlepool Football Club, H'Angus the Monkey. He campaigned for free bananas every day for schoolchildren. To everyone's surprise, he beat all the established candidates, gaining a majority of more than 600 over the Labour candidate. He was re-elected with a majority of over 10,000 in 2005, and Hartlepool now does provide free fruit to schoolchildren.

So far there are only 13 directly elected mayors (including the mayor of London); 20 towns have voted to reject the idea. The positive impact that elected mayors are making will influence more communities to consider having elected mayors.

Contacting your councillor

If you want some advice or have a problem, you can contact your local councillor. You can find out who is your councillor from your local council's website. This should also tell you where and when the councillor holds 'surgeries'. A **surgery** is the name for a private meeting with the councillor.

19

Government in Scotland

Since 1999 Scotland has had its own Parliament that has full responsibility for a range of issues. The Houses of Parliament in Westminster have no say in these areas. This is called the **devolution** of power to Scotland.

Historically Scotland was an independent country. James VI, King of Scots, was next in line to inherit the throne of England when Elizabeth I died and in 1603 he also became James I of England. The two countries were run separately until 1707, when the Act of Union was signed. Both countries were then joined together with a single Parliament in Westminster. Even so, Scotland kept its own legal system and its own educational system. In 1997, in a **referendum**, the people of Scotland voted for their own Parliament, which took power in 1999.

A medal celebrating the Act of Union.

Where does the Scottish Parliament meet?

The Parliament building is opposite the Royal Palace of Holyroodhouse in Edinburgh. It is usually referred to as 'Holyrood'. The building (above) was based on the design of the Spanish architect, Enric Miralles. Not everyone likes it! The main debating chamber is horseshoe-shaped, designed to be less confrontational than the House of Commons.

How is the Parliament elected?

There are 129 Members of the Scottish Parliament (MSPs); 73 are directly elected to represent a constituency. A further 56 are elected by **proportional representation** so that the Parliament reflects the views of all the people better. No single party has obtained a majority of seats in the three

What does the Scottish Parliament do?

It is responsible for:

✔ Agriculture

✔ Culture, arts and leisure

✔ Economic development

✔ Education

✔ Environment

✔ Health

✔ Housing

✔ Legal system and policing

✔ Local government

✔ Social welfare

✔ Transport

It does not have control over:

✘ Defence

✘ Foreign policy

✘ International development

✘ Nationality, immigration and asylum

✘ Social security

✘ Taxation

Shetland Islands

Orkney Islands

Eilean Siar, Comhairle Nan

Moray

Aberdeenshire

Highland

Aberdeen City

Angus

Perth & Kinross

Dundee City

Argyll & Bute

Fife

Stirling

8

City of Edinburgh

1 2 Falkirk

East Lothian

7 6 3

Midlothian

5

North Ayrshire

South Lanarkshire

Scottish Borders

East Ayrshire

South Ayrshire

Dumfries & Galloway

West Lothian

elections held so far. This means the political parties have to work together to make changes.

Local government in Scotland

There are 32 local councils in Scotland. Each authority is responsible for all local government services in its area. In 2007, for the first time, councillors were elected by proportional representation. Most councils are now run by a **coalition** of political parties. There are 1,222 councillors. Councils spend £7.6 billion and employ 230,000 people.

1 West Dunbartonshire
2 East Dunbartonshire
3 North Lanarkshire
4 Glasgow City
5 East Renfrewshire
6 Renfrewshire
7 Inverclyde
8 Clackmannanshire

Government in Wales

Since 1999 Wales has had its own **Assembly** that has some responsibility for a range of issues. Since 2007, it has had limited powers to make laws in its areas of responsibility.

Llywodraeth Cynulliad Cymru
Welsh Assembly Government

The Welsh flag features a red dragon on a white and green background. The Assembly and Assembly Government logos use the dragon. The Welsh flag is one of the oldest in the world.

A strong kingdom of Wales was never established, and by 1284 the English king, Edward I, was able to control Wales. A formal union came about in 1536 and English law was applied to Wales. Whilst a Welsh identity and the Welsh language were retained, political power moved away. In 1997 the people of Wales voted, by a small majority, for the establishment of a National Assembly of Wales, with limited powers. Members of the Assembly form the Welsh Assembly Government.

How is the Assembly elected?

There are 60 Assembly Members (AMs); 40 are elected to represent a constituency. There are a further 20 members who are selected by proportional representation to cover a region of Wales. This mixture of systems makes it hard for any one political party to have a majority. The political parties have to work together to give stable government.

Where does the Assembly meet?

The Assembly building (the Senedd) is on the waterfront at Cardiff Bay. It was designed by the British architect Richard Rogers. The building contains the Siambr, the main debating chamber of the Assembly, and committee meeting rooms for AMs. The Siambr is a circular chamber.

Cynulliad National
Cenedlaethol Assembly for
Cymru **Wales**

What does the National Assembly do?

It is responsible for:

✔ Agriculture

✔ Culture, arts and leisure

✔ Economic development

✔ Education

✔ Environment

✔ Health

✔ Housing

✔ Local government

✔ Social welfare

✔ Transport

✔ Welsh language

It does not have control over:

✘ Defence

✘ Foreign policy

✘ International development

✘ Legal system and policing

✘ Nationality, immigration and asylum

✘ Social security

✘ Taxation

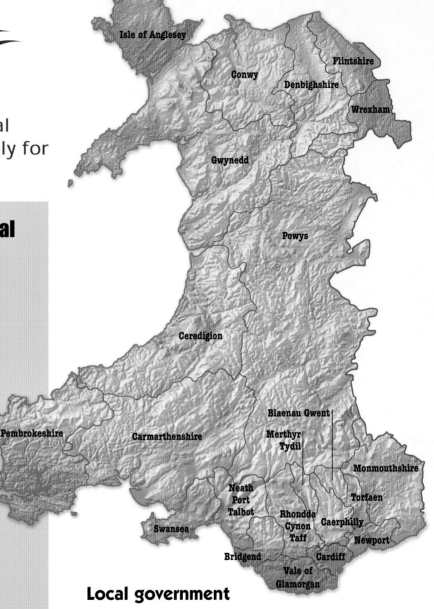

Local government in Wales

There are 22 local councils in Wales, and 1,257 councillors. Each authority has full responsibility for all local services. The councils spend £4 billion – over one third of the total Welsh budget. They employ over 150,000 people.

Government in Northern Ireland

Northern Ireland has had a turbulent recent history. It was a remarkable day on 8 May 2007 when Ian Paisley of the Democratic Unionist Party and Martin McGuinness of Sinn Fein agreed to work together to run a devolved administration in Northern Ireland, with wide-ranging responsibilities.

Northern Ireland Assembly

The logo is based on the flax plant. The six flowers represent the six counties of Northern Ireland. The flax plant was used to make linen, for which Northern Ireland is famous.

Northern Ireland came into existence in 1921 when Ireland was split into two parts, the independent Irish Free State (now the Republic of Ireland) and Northern Ireland, a province of the United Kingdom. In Northern Ireland the Protestant-dominated government ruled from Stormont, their new parliamentary building. Rule from Stormont was suspended in 1972 as a result of conflict between the Protestant and Catholic communities. Westminster ruled directly. The current Northern Ireland Assembly was created in 1999. Power is shared between

Where does the Northern Ireland Assembly meet?

The Assembly meets in a building referred to as Stormont. It was opened in 1932 on an imposing site outside Belfast. The width of the Stormont building is exactly 365 feet, 1 foot for each day of the year. In the Second World War the building was painted black with a mixture of tar and cow manure. It protected the building, but turned out to be very difficult to remove afterwards.

political opponents. It was suspended between 2002 and 2007.

How is the Assembly elected?

There are 108 Members of the Legislative Assembly (MLAs). There are six MLAs for each constituency, and they are elected by proportional representation to reflect the wide range of opinions within Northern Ireland. All major political parties share government power.

Local government in Northern Ireland

There are 26 local councils in Northern Ireland. The councils cover a smaller area than in the rest of the United Kingdom. They also do less. For example, they look after rubbish collection and leisure, but not education, planning, roads and housing. Some of these duties are done by groups of councils working together (such as Education and Library Boards) and some through the Northern Ireland Executive. There are 582 councillors, elected by proportional representation. Councils spend £360 million a year and employ 10,000 people.

The European Union

Britain is a member of the European Union (or EU), a group of 27 European countries that work together to provide economic and social benefits to all the member countries. There are nearly 500 million people in the EU.

What does the EU do?

The EU aims to have common laws and policies in the following areas:

★ Agriculture (through the Common Agricultural Policy) and fisheries.

★ Economic development, including a common currency (the Euro), free movement of goods, common employment practices and common business regulation.

★ Common environmental standards, and a uniform policy on energy use and sustainable development.

★ Human rights and police and judicial cooperation.

★ Common foreign policies on trade, aid, immigration, customs and security.

It applies its policies through European laws and **directives** that are the same throughout the EU. Some countries have opted out of some of these areas: Britain uses the pound not the Euro.

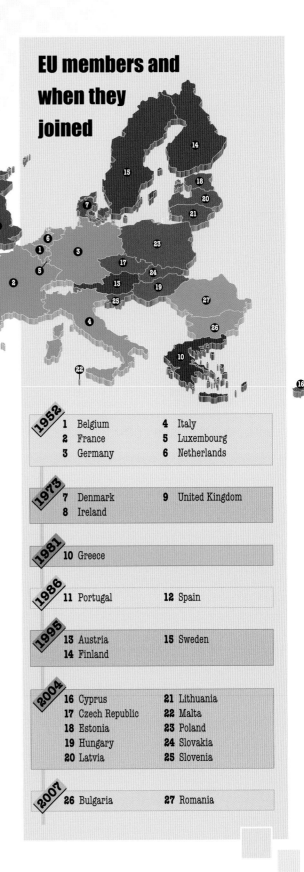

EU members and when they joined

1952			
1	Belgium	4	Italy
2	France	5	Luxembourg
3	Germany	6	Netherlands

1973			
7	Denmark	9	United Kingdom
8	Ireland		

1981		
10	Greece	

1986			
11	Portugal	12	Spain

1995			
13	Austria	15	Sweden
14	Finland		

2004			
16	Cyprus	21	Lithuania
17	Czech Republic	22	Malta
18	Estonia	23	Poland
19	Hungary	24	Slovakia
20	Latvia	25	Slovenia

2007			
26	Bulgaria	27	Romania

The debating chamber of the European Parliament at Strasbourg.

How does the EU work?

There are four important institutions.

The European Parliament

★ Directly elected by voters in the member countries.

★ There are 785 members. Elections are held every five years.

★ Based in Strasbourg and also meets in Brussels.

★ Members of the European Parliament (MEPs) are elected by proportional representation. The UK has 78 members.

★ MEPs work in seven Europe-wide political groups rather than in national groups. Some MEPs oppose the idea of the EU.

The Council of the European Union

★ One minister from each member country, the minister being the appropriate one for the subject under discussion.

★ Jointly makes laws with the European Parliament.

The European Commission

★ The civil servants who administer the EU, sometimes called **Eurocrats**. Most are based in Brussels.

The European Court of Justice

★ The Court rules on any issues relating to European law. It is based in Luxembourg.

EU or UK?

Many people feel the EU has too much control over us, and that we should leave. Others believe the EU makes Europe a safer place and we need to be part of it. What do you think?

The flag

This is the flag of the European Union. The circle of gold stars is meant to represent the united peoples of Europe. There are twelve stars because the number twelve is a symbol of perfection.

Discussion Points

It is easy to take government for granted – and even easier to complain when things do not work or it does something you disagree with. But without it, how would we receive all the services that all levels of government provide? Here are some suggestions for discussion points on the government of Britain (the page numbers indicate where the topic is covered in the book).

- Should Britain have a written constitution that says exactly how we should be governed? (**pages 4–5**)

- Have you watched anything from the House of Commons on television? It can be watched online (**www.bbc.co.uk/parliament**). Look at Prime Minister's Question Time. What did you learn from it? Did it seem relevant to you? (**pages 8–9**)

- No one can decide on the best way to reform the House of Lords. Who do you think should be members and how should they be selected? (**pages 10–11**)

- Look at the charts on **page 13**. Look at the percentage of the vote and the number of MPs elected. Which parties are likely to be happy with the current voting system?

- Why do you think people join political parties? What would happen if there were no political parties? (**pages 14–15**)

- Find out what your local council does. What council services do you use? What would you like your council to do? (**pages 16–17**)

- Voting by proportional representation usually means that no one party can control an elected body. Does this lead to greater cooperation between parties? Look at the examples of devolved government in Scotland, Wales and Northern Ireland. (**pages 20–25**)

- The European Union is liked by some and loathed by others. Is it better to be part of a large group of European nations or are we better at doing everything for ourselves? (**pages 26–27**)

- If you were elected to the House of Commons, what would you want to change?

Websites

There is lots of information on the internet about how Britain is governed. Here are some suggestions of sites that will help you discover more.

To find out more about Parliament, start by visiting **www.explore.parliament.uk** This site provides a guide to how Parliament works.

To get a feel as to what Parliament looks like, there are virtual tours of the House of Commons and the House of Lords:
www.parliament.uk/about/visiting/ virtualtours/commons.cfm
www.parliament.uk/about/visiting/ virtualtours/lords.cfm

If you want to know what is happening in the Houses of Parliament, visit the websites for the Commons and the Lords:
www.parliament.uk/commons,
www.parliament.uk/lords.
You can watch the work of Parliament at **www.bbc.co.uk/parliament**.

To find out more about the government, visit this site provided by 10 Downing Street:
http://youngpeople.pm.gov.uk
For more detailed information on all aspects of government, visit the official government website: **www.direct.gov.uk**

The various voting systems used in different parts of Britain can be confusing. Here is a site that explains how the different systems work:
www.electoral-reform.org.uk/votingsystems /systems.htm

All political parties have websites that give you the chance to see what they are doing and what they believe in. The sites for the main parties are as follows:
www.labour.org.uk
www.conservatives.com
www.libdems.org.uk
www.snp.org
www.plaidcymru.org
www.dup.org.uk
www.sinnfeinassembly.com

All local authorities have websites explaining what they do. This website will help you find your own authority:
www.direct.gov.uk/en/Dl1/Directories/Local councils

The Scottish Parliament, the Assembly of Wales and the Northern Ireland Assembly all have their own websites. These links will provide more information.
www.scottish.parliament.uk/vli/holyrood
www.assemblywales.org/abthome.htm
www.niassembly.gov.uk

And for the European Union, this site provides introductory information:
http://europa.eu/abc/index_en.htm

Note to parents and teachers: Every effort has been made by the Publishers to ensure that these websites are suitable for children, that they are of the highest educational value, and that they contain no inappropriate or offensive material. However, because of the nature of the Internet, it is impossible to guarantee that the contents of these sites will not be altered. We strongly advise that Internet access is supervised by a responsible adult.

Glossary

Act of Parliament A law made by Parliament.

Assembly A name for a meeting place for elected representatives.

assent Agreement. The Monarch gives assent to Acts of Parliament to turn them into law.

ballot paper An official piece of paper used by a voter to mark his or her choice in an election. The ballot paper is put in a ballot box by the voter.

bench A long seat, as in the House of Commons. The front benches are used by ministers, the back benches by ordinary MPs.

Bill In Parliament a proposed new piece of law. When it is approved, it becomes an Act of Parliament.

bribe To pay someone to break the law; in times past voters were bribed to vote for a particular candidate.

by-election When an MP resigns or dies, a by-election is held in the constituency to elect a new MP. By-elections happen between General Elections.

Cabinet The group of senior ministers, led by the Prime Minister, that runs the government.

candidate A person standing for election to Parliament or a local council. The candidate with the most votes wins.

civil servant An official who works for the government and carries out its policies.

coalition When members of different political parties must work together to govern.

Commonwealth A group of countries that used to be ruled directly by Britain.

constituency A geographical area that is represented by one MP. A constituency contains around 70,000 voters.

constitution A description of how a country or organisation works and who is responsible for what.

council An elected body that provides local services.

Council Tax A local tax paid to the council, based on the value of an individual's house.

councillor An elected member of a council.

court A place where law cases are decided.

devolution The passing of power from one level to a lower level. Certain powers have been devolved from the Houses of Parliament to the Scottish Parliament.

directive A regulation made by the European Union that applies in all member states.

donation A gift, usually of money. Donations are made by individuals, companies and trade unions to political parties.

election An event where people select someone for a position by voting for who they want. The person with most votes wins.

Eurocrat Informal term for an official who works for the European Union.

first-past-the-post system An election system where the person or political party with most votes wins and those who do not win take nothing away. Compare this to proportional representation.

General Election An election when all the voters in Britain elect their MP. The political party with the most MPs wins the election and forms the next government.

Hereditary peer A noble who inherits the opportunity to be a member of the House of Lords.

House of Commons The elected chamber of the Houses of Parliament. It is the most important part of Parliament.

House of Lords The second chamber of the Houses of Parliament. Its members are mainly appointed.

independent An election candidate or an elected representative who does not belong to any political party.

inherit To receive something from somebody who has died; it can include money, property or a noble title.

judiciary The legal system and the judges who operate it.

Life peer An appointed member of the House of Lords, chosen because he or she has made a major contribution to this country.

mayor An elected individual who represents a town or city.

Member of Parliament (MP) A person who is elected as a Member of the House of Commons.

minister A politician who is in charge of a government department.

monarchy The system where the head of state of a country is a king or queen.

Parliament The place where elected representatives meet to make the laws of a country.

political party A group of people who believe that the country should be run in a certain way and campaign at elections to get support for their ideas.

Prime Minister The head of the government. The Prime Minister is usually leader of the largest political party in the House of Commons.

proportional representation A system of voting in which each party gains representatives based on the total number of votes cast. Compare with first-past-the-post, where the winner takes all.

referendum A vote in which everyone is asked whether they agree or disagree with a proposal.

Speaker A Member of Parliament elected by MPs to run and keep order in the House of Commons.

stand To put oneself forward for election.

subscription A sum of money paid every year to be a member of an organisation.

surgery The name given to a meeting between an elected representative and individual voters.

trade unionist Someone who looks after the rights of ordinary workers.

vote To indicate on a ballot paper the candidate you wish to elect.

Westminster A term used to describe the Houses of Parliament (because they are in an area of London called Westminster).

Whitehall A term used to describe the government and the civil service (because their main offices are around a street in London called Whitehall).

Index